ALTERNATOR
BOOKS™

MYSTERIES OF THE
EGYPTIAN
PYRAMIDS

Karen Latchana Kenney

Lerner Publications ◆ Minneapolis

To the history detectives of the world,
whose discoveries help us understand our past

Lerner Publications Company
A division of Lerner Publishing Group, Inc.
241 First Avenue North
Minneapolis, MN 55401 USA

For reading levels and more information, look up this title at www.lernerbooks.com.

Main body text set in Aptifer Slab LT Pro Regular 11.5/18.
Typeface provided by Linotype AG.

Library of Congress Cataloging-in-Publication Data

Names: Kenney, Karen Latchana, author.
Title: Mysteries of the Egyptian pyramids / Karen Latchana Kenney.
Description: Minneapolis : Lerner Publications, 2017. | Series: Ancient
    mysteries | Includes bibliographical references and index. |
    Description based on print version record and CIP data provided by
    publisher; resource not viewed.
Identifiers: LCCN 2016044089 (print) | LCCN 2016043074 (ebook) |
    ISBN 9781512449211 (eb pdf) | ISBN 9781512440140 (lb : alk. paper)
Subjects: LCSH: Pyramids—Egypt—Juvenile literature.
Classification: LCC DT63 (print) | LCC DT63 .K46 2017 (ebook) |
    DDC 932—dc23

LC record available at https://lccn.loc.gov/2016044089

Manufactured in the United States of America
1-42276-26133-2/15/2017

TABLE OF CONTENTS

INTRODUCTION
A SECRET CHAMBER?

A toy-train-sized robot inched its way through a small, ancient shaft into Egypt's Great Pyramid on September 17, 2002. An earlier robotic mission into the pyramid had shown that the shaft ended at a stone door. This time, researchers and scientists wanted to find out what was behind the door. They crowded

A technician inspects the robot before sending it into the pyramid's shaft.

inside the Great Pyramid and anxiously watched while TV viewers around the world tuned in. The robot sent live images from its fifty-minute journey through the 200-foot (61-meter) shaft. Gasps from the researchers could be heard as the robot drilled a small hole through the door. Then the robot sent its camera inside.

Famous **Egyptologist** Zahi Hawass was inside the Great Pyramid, commenting during the broadcast. He and a team of seventy people had been waiting for this moment during the mission's yearlong planning. Hawass explained that behind the door was a small empty chamber and another sealed door. It was not quite what the team and viewers had hoped for. So even more questions needed to be answered.

This image shows the robot's view inside the shaft of the Great Pyramid.

Three pyramids stand together on Egypt's Giza Plateau. The one at the back in this image is known as the Great Pyramid.

This forty-five-hundred-year-old pyramid has intrigued people for thousands of years. How was it built? Who built it? What was it used for? Could there be hidden rooms or treasures inside? Historians, **archaeologists**, and scientists are trying to find out.

CHAPTER 1
THE LARGEST PYRAMID

Rising like mountains on the Giza Plateau near Cairo, Egypt, are some of the most studied Egyptian pyramids. These pyramids were built during Egypt's **Old Kingdom**, a period lasting from about 2575 to 2150 BCE. Ancient Egyptians had few tools, and they were not yet using wheels, yet somehow they constructed these massive stone structures.

The Great Pyramid is the largest. It was built for the **pharaoh** Khufu around 2550 BCE. It is 481 feet (147 m) tall, and each side is about 756 feet (230 m) long at the base. The pyramid is made up of more than two million stone blocks that are stacked to form the pointed top of the pyramid.

The Great Pyramid is about as tall as a forty-four-story building.

The Great Pyramid was once covered with smooth, polished limestone. Those who built the pyramids wanted to keep treasure hunters and robbers out. The limestone kept the entrance to the pyramid hidden. Over time, most of the limestone has been torn off or has fallen off. In the ninth century, a governor of Cairo named Abdullah Al Mamun and a team of men dug a tunnel into the side of the pyramid. Their tunnel ran into a passageway inside the pyramid. Then they were able to follow the passageway to find the hidden entrance. They also began to map the pyramid's interior.

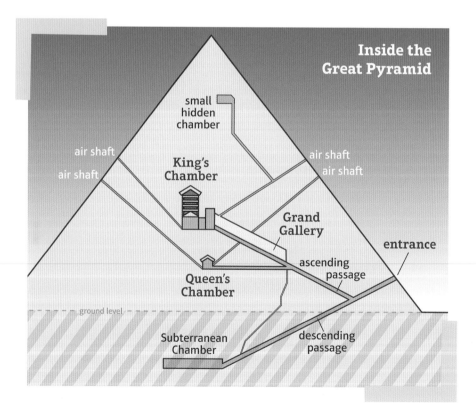

Inside the Great Pyramid

small hidden chamber

air shaft

air shaft

King's Chamber

air shaft

air shaft

Grand Gallery

entrance

ascending passage

Queen's Chamber

ground level

Subterranean Chamber

descending passage

From the entrance, a passage leads down into the pyramid. It ends in the Subterranean Chamber, which is carved right out of the bedrock 98 feet (30 m) below the pyramid. The chamber seems to have never been completed. Another passage leads up into the Queen's Chamber, a 15.5-foot-tall (4.7 m) room with a space that may have held a statue. The orignal explorers of the pyramid named this space the Queen's Chamber, but modern scholars agree that it is unlikely a queen was buried here. Further up the ascending passage is the spectacular Grand Gallery. It is less than 7 feet (2.1 m) wide but is 153 feet (47 m) long, and its ceiling is 28 feet (8.5 m) high. The Grand Gallery is lined by huge granite blocks that form arches.

The Grand Gallery inside the Great Pyramid

Through the Grand Gallery is the King's Chamber, which is made entirely from red granite. Inside is an empty **sarcophagus**. Many believe that the pharaoh Khufu was buried here, but his body has never been found. Some believe it may have been stolen. Two shafts from this room lead to the edges of the pyramid. They may have been built as air shafts for workers or passageways to let Khufu's soul escape.

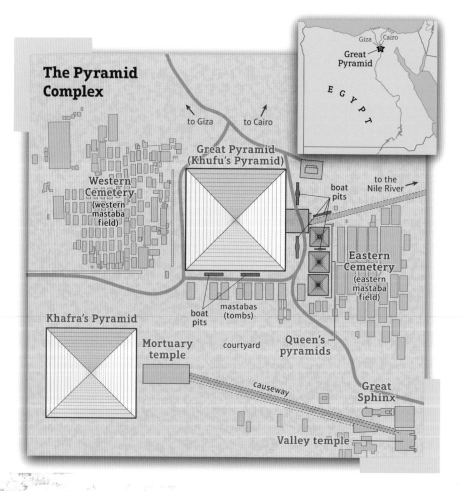

The Pyramid Complex

Giza Cairo
Great Pyramid
E G Y P T

to Giza   to Cairo

Great Pyramid
(Khufu's Pyramid)

Western Cemetery
(western mastaba field)

boat pits

to the Nile River

Eastern Cemetery
(eastern mastaba field)

Khafra's Pyramid

boat pits

mastabas (tombs)

Mortuary temple   courtyard   Queen's pyramids

causeway

Great Sphinx

Valley temple

THE PYRAMID COMPLEX

Like other Egyptian pyramids, the Great Pyramid
is the center of a pyramid complex. The complex,
surrounded by a high wall, also contained several
other pyramids, possibly built for the pharaoh's
queens, and temples. A long passageway may have led
to a temple near the Nile River. Five pits where large
boats were buried were also discovered around the
complex. And cemeteries lay to the east and west of
the pyramid, where relatives and important officials
were buried.

DIP DEEP!

In 1954 Egyptian archaeologist
Kamal el-Mallakh found a pit near
the Great Pyramid. Inside were all
the pieces of an ancient Egyptian
boat. It took a team twenty months
to carefully remove the pieces and
years to put the 144-foot-long (44
m) boat together. This boat may
have brought the pharaoh's coffin
to the pyramid complex. Or it may
be symbolic of Khufu's journey to
the afterlife.

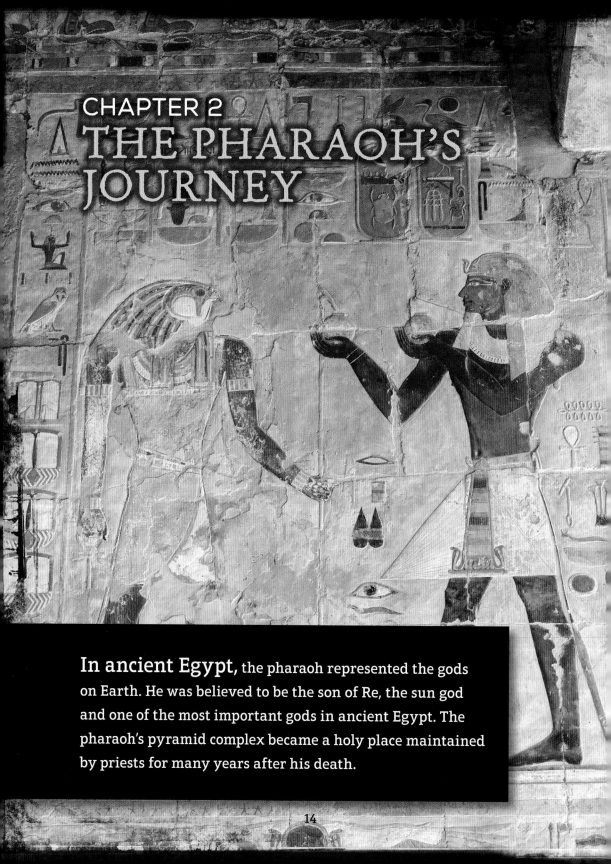

CHAPTER 2
THE PHARAOH'S JOURNEY

In ancient Egypt, the pharaoh represented the gods on Earth. He was believed to be the son of Re, the sun god and one of the most important gods in ancient Egypt. The pharaoh's pyramid complex became a holy place maintained by priests for many years after his death.

According to ancient Egyptian belief, death was the beginning of a journey. At death a pharaoh split into two: his life force, called *ka*, and his soul, called *ba*. He needed to change into his spirit state, *akh*, to reach the afterlife. The pharaoh's body was **mummified** and underwent elaborate rituals before being placed inside a **tomb**. Once inside, Egyptians believed, the pharaoh transformed and rose to rule in the afterlife.

We know about these beliefs from the Pyramid Texts, **hieroglyphs** written inside pyramids built after the Great Pyramid. They describe the pyramid complex, the pharaoh's burial, and burial ceremonies.

Egyptologist Gaston Maspero first found the hieroglyphs known as the Pyramid Texts in 1881. The oldest of these texts is from around 2400-2300 BCE.

ANCIENT TOMBS?

Despite these texts, some people do not believe the Great Pyramid was a tomb since a mummy was not found inside. There have been many different theories about the Great Pyramid. Some say it was a power plant, others believe it was a place to observe the sky, and some even think it was a structure to guide alien spacecraft. But most historians say that the pyramids were built to be tombs. This is because the shape of the pyramids developed from the Egyptian mastaba, a tomb with a burial chamber below and a raised

The entrance to an ancient Egyptian mastaba

level aboveground. The earliest known pyramid was built for the pharaoh Djoser. It looks like five stacked mastabas, so it is known as a step pyramid. Some historians say that pharaohs may have built several pyramids or tombs so that robbers would not be able to easily find their bodies.

Ancient graffiti inside the Great Pyramid also provides evidence that the pyramid was built as a tomb for Khufu. Egyptologist R. Howard Vyse found the graffiti in 1837 by blasting through the roof of the King's Chamber with dynamite. The graffiti, which contained Khufu's name, was probably written by workers who built the pyramid.

MYTH ALERT!

Many people believe that Egyptian pyramids are filled with ancient treasures. But so far, the Great Pyramid is pretty plain inside. The walls are bare, and only a few hieroglyphs have been found. Few items have been found inside. Many other ancient Egyptian tombs have carved scenes on the walls, statues, and other art. Some people think that this means the Great Pyramid was not built as a tomb.

CHAPTER 3
BUILDING THE GREAT PYRAMID

Perhaps one of the greatest mysteries surrounding the Great Pyramid is how this great structure was built without modern tools. Its base is almost perfectly level. Its sides face north, south, east, and west. Building something so precise requires complex engineering and exact measurements.

The stars or the sun may have helped ancient engineers make a reference line aligned to the north. They could then use that line to mark a square base on the ground. They may have also dug trenches and filled them with water. The water would have provided a level reference to help the Egyptians make the land around and under the pyramid flat.

Ancient Egyptians may have used the North Star as a reference for measuring and building the pyramids.

Archaeologists found a horseshoe-shaped limestone quarry on the plateau. Using a map that showed elevation, they calculated the approximate volume of stone removed from the quarry. They compared this figure to the volume of the pyramid, and the numbers were almost equal. Other stones and granite came by boat from distant quarries. Workers may have pulled the blocks over sand made slick with water.

Modern workers still cut limestone blocks from quarries around Cairo.

Tools such as these have been found near the pyramids. When Egyptologists experimented with these tools, they found the tools could easily cut through limestone and granite.

The Egyptians used copper chisels, saws, and hammers to cut limestone rock. Harder granite may have been pounded into shape using other rocks. But how were the blocks lifted into place on the pyramid? In 457 BCE, the ancient Greek historian Herodotus wrote that the Egyptians used machines made of wood to move and lift the blocks. Greek writer Diodorus later wrote about ramps outside of the pyramid.

Historians believe that some sort of ramp was likely used. Ramps have been found at other pyramids, but what the Great Pyramid's ramp looked like is a mystery. It may have wrapped around the pyramid, or it may have been inside the pyramid and later sealed off.

A ramp made of mud bricks stands near a small pyramid in Egypt.

DIG DEEP!

In October 2015, a science mission known as Scan Pyramids launched. Those in charge of the mission planned to create 3-D maps and images of the inside of the pyramid using technology such as lasers and **infrared** that do not disturb the pyramids. Another technology can show the difference between rock and empty spaces. These technologies may reveal empty spaces inside the pyramids and answer questions about how the pyramids were built. In 2016 the team announced that they may have found two empty spaces in the pyramid.

Many people believe that the pyramids were built by slaves. But archaeologists think well-paid and highly skilled workers made the pyramids. There may have been as many as twenty thousand to thirty thousand laborers at a time. Two cities were found near the Great Pyramid, and archaeologists uncovered bakeries and fish and cattle bones. This was not typical food for slaves. Rather, these workers were well fed. And papyrus records found in 2013, written by pyramid workers, show how much the workers were paid and fed.

CHAPTER 4

MODERN MYSTERIES

For hundreds of years, tourists have come to Egypt to see the pyramids. Greek authors listed the Great Pyramid as one of the Seven Wonders of the Ancient World. It is the only one of those ancient wonders to still exist, and it still amazes those who visit.

MYTH ALERT!

Does a curse fall upon people who disturb tombs of the pharaohs? In 1922 archaeologists found the tomb of the pharaoh Tutankhamen in Thebes, Egypt. The night they entered the tomb, a snake killed the pet canary of the head archaeologist, Howard Carter. Within seven years, twelve people who had been in the tomb with Carter were dead. But researchers don't believe a curse killed the people. It was likely just a series of terrible coincidences.

Tutankhamen's tomb

These days, the ancient Giza pyramids are surrounded on three sides by the large city of Cairo, and modern life buzzes by. In 2011 Egypt had a political revolution, and violence broke out in Cairo. Since then fewer tourists have visited Egypt, so less money comes into the country. That means less government money is available for studying and preserving the country's ancient sites.

A view of modern Cairo

Many people continue to explore the pyramids and study their secrets.

STILL SEARCHING

In 2011 a group of scientists sent another robot into the shaft in the Great Pyramid. This time, the robot had a flexible camera to see around corners. Images from the robot showed red hieroglyphs and carved lines in the rock. These markings were probably left by pyramid workers. They may say what the shaft was built for. But the team needs to decode the hieroglyphs to be sure.

In the future, new technology and studies could unlock ancient secrets about the Great Pyramid. Scientists might discover new chambers or a hidden ramp system. But some mysteries about these great ancient structures will never be solved.

SCIENCE SPOTLIGHT
SPACE ARCHAEOLOGY

Space archaeology doesn't sound like a real job, does it? But it's the field archaeologist Sarah Parcak *(below)* studies. She uses satellite images to find ancient sites that have been buried over time. Unusual plant growth or other features of the landscape can show the distinct lines of human-made structures below the ground's surface.

So far, Parcak has found seventeen sites that may hide buried Egyptian pyramids, as well as thousands of sites that may be tombs. In 2016 she was awarded a $1 million TED (Technology, Entertainment, and Design) Prize for her work. She plans to use the money to find even more ancient sites around the world.

Timeline

2613 to 2181 BCE	Pyramid building in Egypt is at its height.
2550	The Great Pyramid's construction is finished.
457	Ancient Greek historian Herodotus writes about machines the Egyptians used to build the pyramids.
1837 CE	Egyptologist R. Howard Vyse finds graffiti containing Khufu's name on the roof of the King's Chamber.
1881	The Pyramid Texts, which explain Egyptian religious beliefs, are discovered.
1954	Archaeologist Kamal el-Mallakh finds a boat pit by the Great Pyramid. He removes pieces from the pit and rebuilds the boat.
2002	A robotic mission explores an unknown area of the Queen's Chamber of the Great Pyramid.
2016	The Scan Pyramids project announces that an area of the Great Pyramid may contain a previously unknown cavity.

GLOSSARY

archaeologists: scientists who study past human life by examining ancient tools, bones, and other artifacts

Egyptologist: a person who studies ancient Egyptian artifacts

hieroglyphs: pictures that are symbols for words, used by ancient Egyptians as writing

infrared: a wavelength of light that cannot be seen by the human eye

mummified: preserved by treating with oils and wrapping in strips of cloth

Old Kingdom: also known as the Age of the Pyramids, a period in Egypt's history lasting from about 2575 to 2150 BCE. This period is known for being a time of strong government and economy.

pharaoh: a king in ancient Egypt

sarcophagus: an ancient stone coffin

tomb: a grave, a room, or a building that holds dead bodies

FURTHER INFORMATION

BBC Bitesize: Ancient Egypt Videos
http://www.bbc.co.uk/education/topics/zg87xnb/videos/1

Bower, Tamara. *The Mummy-Makers of Egypt*. New York: Seven Stories, 2015.

The Children's University of Manchester: Ancient Egypt
http://www.childrensuniversity.manchester.ac.uk/interactives/history/egypt/

Doeden, Matt. *Tools and Treasures of Ancient Egypt*. Minneapolis: Lerner Publications, 2014.

Duke, Shirley. *Pyramids of Egypt*. Vero Beach, FL: Rourke Educational Media, 2015.

National Geographic Kids: Ten Facts about Ancient Egypt
http://www.ngkids.co.uk/history/ten-facts-about-ancient-egypt

National Geographic Society: Explore a Pyramid
http://nationalgeographic.org/education/multimedia/interactive/maps-tools-explore-pyramid/

Raum, Elizabeth. *Egyptian Pyramids*. Mankato, MN: Amicus, 2014.

Time for Kids: Egypt Timeline
http://www.timeforkids.com/destination/egypt/history-timeline

INDEX

PHOTO ACKNOWLEDGMENTS

The images in this book are used with the permission of: © Gordan/Shutterstock. com (grunge border texture); © mihtiander/Deposit Photos, p. 1; © Kenneth Garrett/ National Geographic/Getty Images, pp. 4–5; © Patrick CHAPUIS/Gamma-Rapho/ Getty Images, p. 6; © iStockphoto.com/pabst_ell, p. 7; © Mark Brodkin Photography/ Getty Images, p. 8; © Robster1/Wikimedia Commons (Public Domain), p. 9; © Laura Westlund/Independent Picture Service, p. 10; © Jochen Schlenker/robertharding/ Alamy, p. 11; © Laura Westlund/Independent Picture Service, p. 12; © Noelia Moran/ Alamy, p. 14; © Arash James Iravan/Getty Images, p. 15; © Jim Henderson/Alamy, p. 16; © frans lemmens/Alamy, p. 18; © Bojan Brecelj/Corbis/Getty Images, p. 19; © Amr Sayed/APA Images/ZUMA Wire/Alamy, p. 20; © S. Vannini/De Agostini Picture Library/Getty Images, p. 21; © Mike P Shepherd/Alamy, p. 22; © Janzig/ Egypt/Alamy, p. 24; © CRIS BOURONCLE/AFP/Getty Images, p. 25; © Chris Ison/PA Images/Alamy, p. 26; © frans lemmens/Alamy, p. 27; © Hilary Swift/The New York Times/Redux, p. 28.

Front cover: mihtiander/Deposit Photos; © Gordan/Shutterstock.com (grunge border texture).